Cor

MW00471036

4

Introduction

The celebration of the Eucharist is the heart of the life of the Catholic. The rest of the sacraments, and the life and the ministry of the Church as a whole, derive their meaning and purpose from the Eucharist because Christ Himself is our Eucharist, our Passover, our Living Bread, the source of all our goodness. From His Body, brought to life by the Holy Spirit, all men draw life, and the whole created universe is offered to the Father.

The celebration of the Eucharist outside the Holy Sacrifice of the Mass springs from and directs Christians back to the Mass itself. During Mass the sacrifice of His life, which is made by Christ, the Lord, is one with the life-giving sacrament by which, in the form of bread and wine, He is present with us. After Mass, in church and oratory, He is still God-with-us by the same sacramental presence. For this reason it is understood that when the faithful honor the Blessed Sacrament, they are offering true worship to the one, true God.

This booklet is intended to be a devotional aid to the pastor and his parishioners, deepening their faith in the Eucharist and helping them become living witnesses to the presence of Christ in our world.

Father James F. Seculoff

Directions from 'Holy Communion and Worship of the Eucharist Outside Mass'

[Note: The material in this section and others in this work is excerpted verbatim, paraphrased, or otherwise adapted from the aforementioned source, as applicable.]

FORMS OF WORSHIP OF THE HOLY EUCHARIST (Nos. 79, 80, 81)

The eucharistic sacrifice is the source and culmination of the whole Christian life. Both private and public devotion toward the eucharist, therefore, including devotion outside Mass, are strongly encouraged when celebrated according to the regulations of lawful authority.

In the arrangement of devotional services of this kind, the liturgical seasons should be taken into account. Devotions should be in harmony with the sacred liturgy in some sense, take their origin from the liturgy, and lead the people back to the liturgy.

When the faithful honor Christ present in the sacrament, they should remember that this presence is derived from the sacrifice and is directed toward sacramental and spiritual communion.

The same piety which moves the faithful to eucharistic adoration attracts them to a deeper participation in the paschal mystery. It makes them respond gratefully to the gifts of Christ who by his humanity continues to pour divine life upon the members of his body. Living with Christ the Lord, they achieve a close familiarity with him and in his presence pour out their hearts for themselves and for those dear to them; they pray for peace and for the salvation of the world. Offering their entire lives with Christ to the Father in the Holy Spirit, they draw from this wondrous exchange an increase of faith, hope and love. Thus they nourish the proper disposition to celebrate the memorial of the Lord as devoutly as possible and to receive frequently the bread given to us by the Father.

The faithful should make every effort to worship Christ the Lord in the sacrament, depending upon the circumstances of their own life. Pastors should encourage them in this by example and word.

Prayer before Christ the Lord sacramentally present extends the union with Christ which the faithful have reached in communion. It renews the covenant which in turn moves them to maintain in their lives what they have received by faith and by sacraments. They should try to lead their whole lives with the strength derived from the heavenly food, as they share in the death and resurrection of the Lord. Everyone should be concerned with good deeds and with pleasing God so that he or she may imbue the world with the Christian spirit and be a witness of Christ in the midst of human society.

REGULATIONS FOR EXPOSITION OF THE HOLY EUCHARIST (Nos. 84, 85, 89, 91, 92)

a. A single genuflection is made in the presence of the blessed sacrament, whether reserved in the tabernacle or exposed for public adoration.

b. (i) For exposition of the blessed sacrament in the monstrance, four to six candles are lighted, as at Mass, and incense is used.
(ii) For exposition of the blessed sacrament in the ciborium, at least two candles should be lighted, and incense may be used.

c. Exposition which is held exclusively for the giving of benediction is prohibited.

d. The ordinary minister for exposition of the eucharist is a priest or deacon.

e. The priest or deacon should wear a white cope and humeral veil to give the blessing at the end of adoration, when the exposition takes place with the monstrance; in the case of exposition in the ciborium, the humeral veil should be worn.

ADORATION (No. 95)

During the exposition there should be prayers, songs, and readings to direct the attention of the faithful to the worship of Christ the Lord.

To encourage a prayerful spirit, there should be readings from scripture with a homily or brief exhortations to develop a better understanding of the eucharistic mystery. It is also desirable for the people to respond to the word of God by singing and to spend some periods of time in religious silence.

BENEDICTION (Nos. 97-99)

Toward the end of the exposition the priest or deacon goes to the altar, genuflects and kneels. Then a hymn or other eucharistic song is sung. Meanwhile the minister, while kneeling, incenses the sacrament if the exposition has taken place with the monstrance.

Afterward the minister rises and sings or says:
Let us pray.

After a brief period of silence, the minister continues:
Lord Jesus Christ,
you gave us the eucharist
as the memorial of your suffering and death.
May our worship of this sacrament of your body
and blood
help us to experience the salvation you won for us

**and the peace of the kingdom
where you live with the Father and the Holy Spirit,
one God, for ever and ever.**
All respond:
Amen.

[Other prayers, such as the following, may be chosen.]
**Lord our God,
you have given us the true bread from heaven.
In the strength of this food
may we live always by your life
and rise in glory on the last day.
We ask this through Christ our Lord.**

Or:
**Lord,
give to our hearts
the light of faith and the fire of love,
that we may worship in spirit and in truth
our God and Lord, present in this sacrament,
who lives and reigns for ever and ever.**

*After the prayer the priest or deacon puts on the
humeral veil, genuflects, and takes the monstrance or
ciborium. He makes the sign of the cross over the people
with the monstrance or ciborium, in silence.*

REPOSITION (No. 100)

After the blessing the priest or deacon who gave the
blessing, or another priest or deacon, replaces the
blessed sacrament in the tabernacle and genuflects.
Meanwhile the people may sing or say an acclamation,
and the minister then leaves.

Prefatory Note

The people of God are to take part in the singing of all hymns. The parts prefixed with "Pr." are said by the priest or deacon; those prefixed with "P." are said by the people; those prefixed with "R." are recited or sung by a member of the congregation appointed by the priest or deacon in charge.

For the sake of variation the prayers and hymns may follow a different sequence and other prayers or hymns may be substituted. So that you, the people of God, will recite these prayers with clarity and dignity, please observe all pauses (indicated by the symbol ~).

The first part of the booklet contains prayers and hymns for an hour of adoration. The second part contains other prayers and hymns proper for the Solemn Annual Exposition (formerly The Forty Hours Devotion).

The Appendices contain a sample service for Eucharistic Exposition and Benediction with Evening Prayer and a model service for Eucharistic Exposition and Benediction provided by the National Conference of Catholic Bishops, Bishops' Committee on the Liturgy.

PART I

Exposition of the Blessed Sacrament

O Salutaris*

O Salutaris Hostia,
Quae coeli pandis ostium!
Bella premunt hostilia;
Da robur fer auxilium.
Uni Trinoque Domino
Sit sempeterna gloria;
Qui vitam sine termino
Nobis donet in patria.
Amen.

*O Saving Victim

O saving Victim, open wide,
The gate of heaven to man below,
Our foes press on from every side;
Your aid supply, Your strength bestow,
To Your great name be endless praise,
Immortal Godhead, One in Three,
O grant us endless length of days
In our true native land with Thee.
Amen.

1 ✧ Intention

All: **In the name of the Father ~ and of the Son, ~ and of the Holy Spirit. Amen.**

Pr. Open, O Lord, our mouths ~

P. **To bless Your holy Name; ~ cleanse our hearts ~ from all vain, evil, and distracting thoughts; ~ enlighten our understanding. ~ Inflame our wills; ~ that we may worthily, ~ attentively, and**

devoutly ~ spend this hour ~ in the presence of
Your divine Majesty; ~ through Christ our Lord.
~ Amen.

2 ✧ Opening Prayer

Pr. Come Holy Spirit, ~ fill the hearts of Your faithful.

P. **And kindle in them the fire of Your love.**

Pr. O Lord, ~ Jesus Christ ~

P. **Who has promised ~ that wherever two or three
~ shall be gathered in Your name, ~ You will be
in the midst of them; ~ look down with
compassion, ~ love and mercy upon us ~ who
are now united before You ~ in the lowliness of
our hearts ~ to adore Your Sacred Presence, ~ in
the desire to make it known and loved by all. ~
Stay in our midst, ~ sweet Jesus. ~ Fill our
hearts with Your blessings, ~ inflame them with
Your love. ~ O Jesus, ~ humbly kneeling in Your
Presence, ~ and united with all the faithful on
earth, ~ and the saints in heaven, ~ we adore
You, ~ true God and true Man, ~ here present in
the Eucharist.**

**Lord Jesus, ~ we desire during this hour ~ to
adore You, ~ to thank You, ~ to renew our
sorrow for sin, ~ and to ask for all the graces ~
of which we stand in need. ~ We also desire to
make reparation ~ for our own coldness toward
You ~ in the Sacrament of Your love; ~ for the
ingratitude and sins of others, ~ especially for
the outrages and sacrileges offered You ~ in the
most Holy Sacrament.**

**We offer this Holy Hour ~ for the general
intention for which we make it ~ (that God
might bless this parish) ~ and for our own**

particular intentions. Grant us the grace, dear
Jesus, ~ to spend this hour ~ for Your greater
honor and glory.

O Sacramental Jesus, ~ be our Mediator with
Your heavenly Father. ~ Strengthen our
weakness; ~ confirm our resolutions; ~ make us
love You more and more; ~ grant that nothing in
life or death ~ may ever separate us from You.
Amen.

3 ✧ Invitation — *partly from Psalm 94*

Pr. O Sacrament most holy, ~ O Sacrament divine.

**P. All praise and all thanksgiving ~ be every
moment Thine.**

Pr. Come, ~ let us praise our Eucharistic Lord, ~ the
King of everlasting glory.

**P. Come, ~ let us praise our Eucharistic Lord, ~ the
King of everlasting glory.**

Pr. Come ~ let us sing unto the Lord with joy; ~ to
God, our Savior, ~ let us raise a song of praise; ~
before His face let us offer thanks, ~ and raise our
hearts to Him ~ in psalms of jubilee.

**P. Come, ~ let us praise our Eucharistic Lord, ~ the
King of everlasting glory.**

Pr. Because the Lord is great, ~ the God of might, ~ a
mighty King above all gods; ~ His people He will not
disdain; ~ for in His hand are all the ends of the
earth ~ and on the mountain heights His eye does
rest.

**P. Come, ~ let us praise our Eucharistic Lord, ~ the
King of everlasting glory.**

Pr. The sea is His, ~ for He created it; ~ the land His
hands have formed. ~ Come, ~ in adoration let us
bend the knee before our God; ~ for truly He is our

Lord, ~ our God; ~ and we His people ~ are the sheep of His pasture.

P. **Come, ~ let us praise our Eucharistic Lord, ~ the King of everlasting glory.**

Pr. O Sacrament, most holy, ~ O Sacrament divine.

P. **All praise and all thanksgiving ~ be every moment Thine.**

4 ✧ Acts of Adoration

Pr. Jesus, our God ~

P. **We adore You, ~ here present in the Blessed Sacrament of the Altar, ~ where You wait day and night, ~ to be our comfort ~ while we look forward to Your unveiled Presence in heaven. ~ Jesus, our God, ~ we adore You in all places ~ where the Blessed Sacrament is reserved, ~ especially where You are little honored, ~ and where sins are committed against this Sacrament of Love. ~ Jesus, our God, ~ we adore You for all time, ~ past, present and future, ~ for every soul that ever was, ~ is, or shall be created. ~ Jesus, our God, ~ Who for us has endured hunger and cold, ~ labor and fatigue, ~ we adore You. ~ Jesus, our God, ~ Who for our sake has deigned to subject Yourself ~ to the humiliation of temptation, ~ to the perfidy and defection of friends, ~ to the scorn of Your enemies, ~ we adore You. ~ Jesus, our God Who for us has endured the buffetings of Your Passion, ~ the scourging ~ the crown of thorns, ~ the heavy weight of the Cross, ~ we adore You. ~ Jesus, our God, ~ Who for our salvation, ~ and that of all mankind ~ was cruelly nailed to the Cross, ~ hung thereon for three long hours in**

bitter agony ~ we adore You. ~ Jesus, our God, ~ who for love of us, ~ did institute this Blessed Sacrament ~ does offer Yourself daily for the sins of men, ~ we adore You. ~ Jesus, our God, ~ Who in Holy Communion becomes the food of our souls, ~ we adore You.

Jesus, I live for you ~ Jesus, I die for you, ~ Jesus, I am yours ~ in life and in death. Amen.

5 ✧ Hymn

6 ✧ Scripture Reading — *Ezekiel 34:11-16*

R. A reading from the book of the Prophet Ezekiel.

I will take care of my flock.

Thus says the Lord God: I myself will look after and tend my sheep. As a shepherd tends his flock when he finds himself among his scattered sheep, so will I tend my sheep. I will rescue them from every place where they were scattered when it was cloudy and dark. I will lead them out from among the peoples and gather them from the foreign lands; I will bring them back to their own country and pasture them upon the mountains of Israel (in the land's ravines and all its inhabited places). In good pastures will I pasture them, and on the mountain heights of Israel shall be their grazing ground. There they shall lie down on good grazing ground, and in rich pastures shall they be pastured on the mountains of Israel. I myself will pasture my sheep; I myself will give them rest, says the Lord God. The lost I will seek out, the strayed I will bring back, the injured I will bind up, the sick I will heal (but the sleek and the strong I will destroy), shepherding them rightly.

7 ✧ Responsorial Psalm — *Isaiah 12:2-6*

R. You will draw water joyfully
from the springs of salvation.

Pr. God indeed is my savior;
I am confident and unafraid.
My strength and my courage is the Lord,
and he has been my savior.
With joy you will draw water
at the fountain of salvation.

P. **You will draw water joyfully
from the springs of salvation.**

Pr. Give thanks to the Lord, acclaim his name;
among the nations make known his deeds,
proclaim how exalted is his name.

P. **You will draw water joyfully
from the springs of salvation.**

Pr. Sing praise to the Lord for his glorious achievement;
let this be known throughout all the earth.
Shout with exultation, O city of Zion,
for great in your midst
is the Holy One of Israel!

P. **You will draw water joyfully
from the springs of salvation.**

8 ✧ Scripture Reading — *John 10:11-18*

Pr. A reading from the holy gospel according to John.
A good shepherd is ready to die for his flock.
Jesus said to his disciples:
"I am the good shepherd;
the good shepherd lays down his life for the sheep.
The hired hand who is no shepherd,
nor owner of the sheep,
catches sight of the wolf coming
and runs away, leaving the sheep

to be snatched and scattered by the wolf.
This is because he works for pay;
he has no concern for the sheep.
I am the good shepherd;
I know my sheep
and my sheep know me
in the same way that the Father knows me
and I know the Father;
for these sheep I will give my life.
I have other sheep
that do not belong to this fold;
I must lead them, too,
and they shall hear my voice.
There shall be one flock then, one shepherd.
The Father loves me for this:
that I lay down my life
to take it up again.
No one takes it from me;
I lay it down freely.
I have power to lay it down,
and I have power to take it up again.
This command I received from my Father."

9 ✧ Homily and (or) silent reflection

At this point the priest may give a homily or a meditation, during which the people are seated. If no homily or meditation is given, the following prayers may be said.

10 ✧ Offering

P. **Take my life, and let it be**
    consecrated, Lord, to Thee;
    Take my moments and my days,
    let them flow in ceaseless praise;
    Take my hands and let them work

duty's bidding never shirk.
Take my feet and let them be
swift and dutiful to Thee.
Take my voice and let it sing
Your eternal love, my King;
Take my lips and let them be
filled with messages from Thee;
Take my intellect and use
every power as You shall choose;
Take my will and make it flee
all that gives offense to Thee.
Take my heart, it is Your own.
let it be Your royal throne;
Take my love, my Lord, I pour
at your feet its treasure store;
Take myself, all that is mine
To be forever only Thine.

11 ✧ Thanksgiving

Pr. O my God ~

P. I thank You for all the favors ~ You have given
me. ~ I give You thanks from the bottom of my
heart ~ for having created me, ~ for all the joys
of life ~ and its sorrows, too, ~ for the home You
gave me, ~ for the loved ones with which You
have surrounded me, ~ for the friends I have
made through life.

My Lord God, ~ I thank You for guarding me
always, ~ and keeping me safe; ~ I thank You for
forgiving me so often ~ in the Sacrament of
Penance; ~ for offering Yourself in the Holy Mass
~ with all of Your infinite merits to the Father
for me; ~ for coming to me in Holy Communion
~ in spite of the coldness of my welcome; ~ for

Your patient waiting in the adorable sacrament of the altar.

My Jesus, ~ I thank You for having lived, ~ suffered, and died for me ~ I thank You for Your love. ~ I thank You, Lord, ~ for preparing a place for me in heaven, ~ where I hope to be happy with You ~ and to thank You for all eternity. Amen.

12 ✧ Prayer for Priests

Pr. O Jesus Eternal Priest ~

P. Keep Thy priests within the shelter of Thy Sacred Heart, ~ where none may touch them.

Keep unstained their anointed hands, ~ which daily touch Thy Sacred Body.

Keep unsullied their lips, ~ daily purpled with Thy Precious Blood.

Keep pure and unworldly their hearts, ~ sealed with the sublime mark of the priesthood.

Let Thy love surround them ~ from the world's contagion.

Bless their labors with abundant fruit, ~ and may the souls to whom they minister ~ be their consolation here ~ and their everlasting crown hereafter. ~ Amen.

(Compiled by Rev. S. J. Mauer.)

13 ✧ Hymn

14 ✧ The Rosary

The celebrant invites the participants to meditate on the Joyful, Sorrowful, or Glorious Mysteries while leading them in praying the Rosary.

Joyful Mysteries

1. The Annunciation — The angel tells Mary she is to be the Mother of the Savior.
2. The Visitation — Mary, in charity, goes to visit her cousin Elizabeth.
3. The Nativity — Jesus is born to Mary.
4. The Presentation of the Child Jesus in the Temple — Mary and Joseph take the child to the temple to fulfill the law.
5. The Finding of the Child Jesus in the Temple — After three days of searching, Mary and Joseph find Jesus.

Sorrowful Mysteries

1. The Agony in the Garden — Our sins weigh upon Jesus.
2. The Scourging at the Pillar — Jesus is scourged for our sins.
3. The Crowning with Thorns — Thorns pierce our Lord's head.
4. Jesus Carries the Cross — He carries it to Calvary for us.
5. The Crucifixion — For three hours Jesus suffers intensely on the cross.

Glorious Mysteries

1. Resurrection — Jesus rises from the dead.
2. The Ascension — After forty days Jesus ascends bodily to heaven.
3. The Descent of the Holy Spirit — The Third Person of the Trinity comes to earth in the form of tongues of fire.
4. The Assumption — Mary's body is taken into heaven.
5. The Crowning of the Blessed Virgin — Mary is crowned queen of heaven and earth.

15 ✦ Hymn

16 ✦ Litany of the Sacred Heart

Pr. Lord, have mercy on us.

P. **Christ, have mercy on us.**

Pr. Lord, have mercy on us. Christ, hear us.

P. **Christ, graciously hear us.**

Pr. God the Father of Heaven.

P. **Have mercy on us.** *(Same response for the following invocations.)*

Pr. God the Son, Redeemer of the world,

God the Holy Spirit,

Holy Trinity, one God,

Heart of Jesus, Son of the Eternal Father,

Heart of Jesus, formed by the Holy Spirit, in the womb of the Virgin Mother,

Heart of Jesus, substantially united to the Word of God,

Heart of Jesus, of infinite majesty,

Heart of Jesus, holy temple of God,

Heart of Jesus, tabernacle of the Most High,

Heart of Jesus, house of God and gate of heaven,

Heart of Jesus, burning furnace of charity,

Heart of Jesus, abode of justice and love,

Heart of Jesus, full of goodness and love,

Heart of Jesus, abyss of all virtues,

Heart of Jesus, most worthy of all praise,

Heart of Jesus, King and center of all hearts,

Heart of Jesus, in Whom are all the treasures of wisdom and knowledge,

Heart of Jesus, in Whom dwells the fullness of Divinity,

Heart of Jesus, in Whom the Father was well pleased,

Heart of Jesus, of Whose fullness we have all
    received,
Heart of Jesus, desire of the everlasting hills,
Heart of Jesus, patient and full of mercy,
Heart of Jesus, enriching all who invoke you,
Heart of Jesus, fountain of life and holiness,
Heart of Jesus, propitiation for our sins,
Heart of Jesus, loaded down with reproaches,
Heart of Jesus, bruised for our offenses,
Heart of Jesus, obedient unto death,
Heart of Jesus, pierced with a lance,
Heart of Jesus, source of all consolation,
Heart of Jesus, our life and resurrection,
Heart of Jesus, our peace and reconciliation,
Heart of Jesus, victim of sin,
Heart of Jesus, salvation of those who trust in You,
Heart of Jesus, hope of those who die in You,
Heart of Jesus, delight of all the saints,

Pr. Lamb of God, you take away the sins of the world,

P. **Spare us, O Lord.**

Pr. Lamb of God, you take away the sins of the world,

P. **Graciously hear us, O Lord.**

Pr. Lamb of God, you take away the sins of the world,

P. **Have mercy on us.**

Pr. Jesus, meek and humble of heart,

P. **Make our hearts like yours.**

Pr. Let us Pray: O Almighty and Eternal God, ~ look
upon the heart of Your dearly beloved Son, ~ and
upon the praise and satisfaction he offers You ~ in
the name of sinners ~ and for those who seek Your
mercy; ~ be appeased, ~ and grant us pardon ~ in
the name of the same Jesus Christ, ~ Your Son. ~
Who lives and reigns with You, ~ in the unity of the
Holy Spirit, ~ world without end. ~ Amen.

17 ✧ Consecration of the Human Race to the Sacred Heart of Jesus

Pr. O Jesus ~

P. Redeemer of the human race, ~ look down upon us humbly prostrate before Your altar. ~ We are Yours and Yours we wish to be; ~ but to be more surely united with You, ~ behold each one of us freely consecrates himself today ~ to Your Most Sacred Heart. ~ Many indeed have never known You; ~ many, too, despising Your precepts, ~ have rejected You. ~ Have mercy on them all, ~ Most Merciful Jesus, ~ and draw them to Your Sacred Heart. ~ Be King, O Lord, ~ not only of the faithful who have never forsaken You, ~ but also of the prodigal children ~ who have abandoned You. ~ Grant that they may quickly return to their Father's house ~ before they die of wretchedness and hunger. ~ Be King of those who are deceived by erroneous opinions, ~ or whom discord keeps aloof, ~ and call them back to the harbor of truth ~ and unity of faith ~ so that soon there may be but one flock and one shepherd. ~ Grant, O Lord to Your Church, ~ assurance of freedom and immunity from harm; ~ give peace and order to all nations, ~ and make the earth resound from pole to pole with one cry: ~ Praise to the Divine Heart that wrought our salvation; ~ to it be glory and honor forever. ~ Amen.

18 ✧ Promises of Our Lord — *To St. Margaret Mary for Souls Devoted to His Sacred Heart*

Pr. 1   I will give them all the graces necessary in their state of life.

P.   **O Sacred Heart of Jesus ~ grant us the grace ~ to fulfill faithfully ~ the duties of our state of life.**

Pr. 2   I will establish peace in their homes.

P.   **O Sacred Heart of Jesus ~ bless our homes ~ with Your sweet peace.**

Pr. 3   I will comfort them in all their afflictions.

P.   **O Sacred Heart of Jesus ~ console us ~ in the hour of affliction.**

Pr. 4   I will be their secure refuge during life, and above all in death.

P.   **O Sacred Heart of Jesus ~ secure us in Your Sacred Heart ~ and assist us ~ in the hour of our death.**

Pr. 5   I will bestow a great blessing upon all their undertakings.

P.   **O Sacred Heart of Jesus ~ crown our efforts with success.**

Pr. 6   Sinners shall find in My Heart the source and infinite ocean of mercy.

P.   **O Sacred Heart of Jesus ~ show forth to sinners ~ the depth of Your mercy.**

Pr. 7   Tepid souls shall grow fervent.

P.   **O Sacred Heart of Jesus ~ inflame our hearts ~ with zeal for Your kingdom.**

Pr. 8   Fervent souls shall quickly mount to high perfection.

P.   **O Sacred Heart of Jesus ~ aid us to greater perfection.**

Pr. 9   I will bless every place where a picture of My Heart shall be set up and honored.

P. **O Sacred Heart of Jesus ~ let Your Sacred Image ~ bring blessings upon our homes.**

Pr. 10 I will give to priests the gift of touching the most hardened sinners.

P. **O Sacred Heart of Jesus ~ grant the grace of repentance ~ to wayward sinners.**

Pr. 11 Those who shall promote this devotion shall have their names written in My Heart, never to be blotted out.

P. **O Sacred Heart of Jesus ~ engrave our names ~ in Your Sacred Heart.**

Pr. 12 I promise you in the excessive mercy of My Heart, that my all-powerful love will grant to all those who communicate on the First Friday in nine consecutive months, the grace of final perseverance; they shall not die in My disgrace nor without receiving the Sacraments;

P. **O Sacred Heart of Jesus ~ be our solace in death ~ and grant us the grace ~ of final perseverance. Amen.**

19 ✧ Hymn

20 ✧ Prayer for Vocations

O dearest Jesus, Son of the eternal Father and Mary Immaculate, grant to our boys and girls, the generosity necessary to follow your call, and the courage required to overcome all obstacles to their vocation. Give to parents, that faith, love, and spirit of sacrifice, which will inspire them to offer their children to God's service, and cause them to rejoice exceedingly, whenever one of their children is called to the religious life.

Let your example, and that of your blessed Mother

and St. Joseph, encourage both children and parents, and let your grace sustain them. Amen.

21 ✦ An Offering of Self

*From the **Spiritual Exercises** of St. Ignatius of Loyola*

Take, O Lord, into your hands my entire liberty, my memory, my understanding, and my will. All that I am and have, you have given me, and I surrender them to you, to be so disposed in accordance with your holy will.

Give me your love and your grace; with these I am rich enough and desire nothing more.

22 ✦ The Rabboni Prayer

Written by a Jesuit priest just before he died.

Rabboni, when I am dying
How glad I shall be
That the lamp of my life
Has burned out for Thee.

That sorrow has darkened
The path that I trod,
That thorns and not roses
Were strewn o'er the sod.

That anguish of spirit
So often was mine,
Since anguish of spirit
So often was Thine.

My cherished Rabboni,
How glad I shall be
That the lamp of my life
Has burned out for Thee.

23 ✧ Prayer of Loyalty to God

Pr. God the Father, Creator of heaven and earth.

P. **I love you, O my God.** *(Same response for the following invocations.)*

Pr. God the Son, Redeemer of the world,
God, the Holy Spirit,
Holy Trinity, one God,
You, Who are infinite love,
You, Who did first love me,
You, Who command me to love You,
With all my heart,
With all my soul,
With all my mind,
With all my strength,
Above all possessions and honors,
Above all pleasures and enjoyments,
More than myself,
More than anything belonging to me,
More than all my relatives and friends,
More than all men and angels,
Above all created things in heaven and on earth,
Because You are the Sovereign God,
Only for Yourself,
Because You are infinitely worthy of being loved,
Even if You had not promised me heaven,
Even if You had not menaced me with hell,
Even if You should try me with want and
misfortune,
In wealth and poverty,
In prosperity and adversity,
In health and in sickness,
In time and in eternity,
In union with that love wherewith the saints love
You,

In union with that love wherewith the Blessed
    Virgin loves You,
In union with that love wherewith the angels love
    You in heaven,
In union with that love wherewith You love Yourself
    eternally, . . .

24 ✧ Benediction

Tantum Ergo*

Tantum ergo Sacramentum,
Veneremur cernui;
Et antiquum documentum,
Novo cedat ritui:
Praestet fides supplementum
Sensuum defectui.
Genitori, Genitoque,
Laus et jubilatio:
Salus, honor, virtus quoque
Sit et benedictio
Procendenti ab otroque
Compar sit laudatio.
Amen.

Pr. Panem de coelo praestitisti eis (Alleluia).
P. Omne delectamentum in se habentem (Alleluia).

*Down in Adoration Falling

Down in adoration falling
Lo! the Sacred Host we hail;
Lo! o'er ancient forms departing
Newer rites of grace prevail;
Faith for all defects supplying
Where the feeble senses fail.
To the everlasting Father,
And the Son who reigns on high,
With the Holy Spirit proceeding
Forth from each eternally.

Be salvation, honor, blessing
Might and endless majesty. Amen.

Pr. You have given them bread from heaven (Alleluia).

P. Having all sweetness within it (Alleluia).

While the hymn is being sung, the minister, kneeling, incenses the Most Blessed Sacrament if the exposition has taken place with the monstrance.

Afterward the minister rises and sings or says:

Pr. Oremus.

Or:

Pr. Let us pray.

After a brief period of silence, the minister continues (in Latin or in English):

Pr. Deus, qui nobis sub Sacramento mirabili Passionis tuae memoriam reliquisti; tribue, quaesumus, ita nos Corporis et Sanguinis tui sacra mysteria venerari, ut redemptionis tuae fructum in nobis iugiter sentiamus. Qui vivis et regnas in saecula saeculorum.

P. **Amen.**

Or:

Pr. Lord Jesus Christ, you gave us the eucharist as the memorial of your suffering and death. May our worship of this sacrament of your body and blood help us to experience the salvation you won for us and the peace of the kingdom where you live with the Father and the Holy Spirit, one God, for ever and ever.

P. **Amen.**

Other prayers may be chosen:
Lord our God,
in this great sacrament

we come into the presence of Jesus Christ, your Son,
born of the Virgin Mary
and crucified for our salvation.
May we who declare our faith in this fountain of love
    and mercy
drink from it the water of everlasting life.
We ask this through Christ our Lord.
Or:
Lord our God,
may we always give due honor
to the sacramental presence of the Lamb who was
    slain for us.
May our faith be rewarded
by the vision of his glory,
who lives and reigns for ever and ever.

*After the prayer the priest or deacon puts on the
humeral veil, genuflects, and takes the monstrance or
ciborium. He makes the sign of the cross over the people
with the monstrance or ciborium, in silence.*

*After the blessing the priest or deacon who gave the
blessing, or another priest or deacon, replaces the blessed
sacrament in the tabernacle and genuflects. Meanwhile
the people may sing or say an acclamation, and the
minister then leaves.*

25 ✧ The Divine Praises

Pr.   Humbly let us recite the Divine Praises in joy and
        adoration and in reparation for profane language.
        Blessed be God.
        Blessed be His Holy Name.
        Blessed be Jesus Christ, true God and true man.
        Blessed be the Name of Jesus.
        Blessed be His most Sacred Heart.
        Blessed be His most Precious Blood.

Blessed be Jesus in the Most Holy Sacrament of the
altar.
Blessed be the Holy Spirit, the Paraclete.
Blessed be the great Mother of God, Mary most holy.
Blessed be her holy and Immaculate Conception.
Blessed be her glorious assumption.
Blessed be the name of Mary, Virgin and Mother.
Blessed be St. Joseph, her most chaste spouse.
Blessed be God in His angels and in His saints.

Other prayers may be chosen:
Lord,
may this sacrament of new life
warm our hearts with your love
and make us eager
for the eternal joy of your kingdom.
We ask this through Christ our Lord.
Or:
Lord our God,
teach us to cherish in our hearts
the paschal mystery of your Son
by which you redeemed the world.
Watch over the gifts of grace
your love has given us
and bring them to fulfillment
in the glory of heaven.
We ask this through Christ our Lord.

PART II

Solemn Annual Exposition

The Solemn Annual Exposition is a revised form of Forty Hours Devotion, in harmony with the principles set down for the Church by the Second Vatican Council. These introductory notes are drawn from the document "Holy Communion and Worship of the Eucharist Outside Mass," published on June 21, 1973, by the Congregation for Divine Worship.

Time: Suggested time for the Solemn Annual Exposition is around the time of the Feast of Corpus Christi or the months of October or November. Try not to conflict with seasons of Advent, Christmas, Lent, and Easter.

Length: You are encouraged to set aside one, two, or three days to stimulate in your parishioners a deeper awareness of the presence of Christ as well as an invitation to spiritual communion with Him.

Caution: Since it is now forbidden to celebrate a Mass before the exposed Blessed Sacrament, if exposition is prolonged for a day or more, it should be interrupted during the celebration of Mass.

Suggestion: Perhaps a Parish Penitential Service could be scheduled the Friday evening preceding the Solemn Annual Exposition.

Arrange to have a number of persons in church during the hours of exposition. Provide prayer booklets to help the people in their devotions.

Opening of Solemn Annual Exposition

Sunday, Opening Day: Mass of the Sunday or Votive Mass of the Eucharist where permitted. Mass is celebrated as usual (although the host to be used for exposition is consecrated and the use of incense is encouraged) until the prayer after Communion, when it ends.

Exposition and Procession: Exposition begins at the end of the last Mass. A "single" genuflection is always used; "double" genuflections are no longer used in the liturgy.

Sequence: When the prayer after Communion is concluded. . . **(a)** the priest changes to a white cope or remains in his chasuble; **(b)** a monstrance is brought to the altar; **(c)** the deacon or priest places the host in the monstrance and turns it to face the people; **(d)** the priest incenses the Blessed Sacrament; **(e)** the procession now begins to form; **(f)** lights, incense, and the canopy under which the priest walks, while carrying the Blessed Sacrament, should be in accordance with local customs; **(g)** an appropriate hymn (or hymns) in honor of the Eucharist is to be sung during the procession; **(h)** after the procession the monstrance is placed in a prominent position, such as on the altar, and the Blessed Sacrament may be incensed again; **(i)** some time is spent in prayer, then the priest and the people should genuflect and leave.

Or:

The host should be consecrated in the Mass that immediately precedes the exposition and after Communion it should be placed in the monstrance on the altar. The Mass ends with the prayer after Communion, and the concluding rites are omitted. Before the priest leaves, he places the monstrance in a prominent place and incenses it.

Evening Celebration

a. *With Mass:* Several minutes before Mass is to begin, the priest, wearing a surplice and stole, adores the Blessed Sacrament for a short time, and replaces it in the tabernacle. Then the celebration of Mass begins as usual.

b. *When Mass is not celebrated:* The service is usually observed as a Bible Service or Holy Hour.

Bible Service

The following service includes three Scripture themes — Forms A, B, and C — one of which is to be selected for use during the service.

1 ✧ Opening Hymn

2 ✧ Introduction

Pr. Dear Jesus ~

P. I believe that You are really and truly ~ substantially present ~ in the tabernacle before me ~ under the appearance of bread. ~ The sanctuary lamp burns ~ in honor of Your real presence ~ in this Catholic church. ~ I love and adore You profoundly ~ and beg pardon for those who do not love You ~ and do not adore Your presence in this Most Blessed Sacrament. ~ I kneel in Your presence, ~ unworthy as I am, ~ and beg pardon for all the offenses ~ I and others ~ have committed against You. ~ Warm our cold hearts. ~ Grant us peace and happiness ~ in the knowledge that Your abiding love ~ made it possible for us to receive You ~ in Holy Communion ~ and to adore You in this most august sacrament.

O Eucharistic Heart of Jesus, ~ I adore You profoundly. ~ Let the love of Your Sacred Heart ~ radiate the warmth of its fire ~ to enkindle my own poor cold heart. ~ Enlighten the darkness of

my mind. ~ Strengthen the weakness of my will.
~ Bathe me in Your Most Precious Blood ~ which
I now offer to our heavenly Father ~ in union
with the Holy Sacrifice of the Mass ~ being
offered throughout the world.

You know, ~ dear Lord Jesus, ~ that I am here
present before You. ~ You can read the desires of
my heart, ~ You know my problems, ~ my
petitions, ~ my ingratitude. ~ Accept at least ~
my weak desire to love You more, ~ and may I
never offend You. ~ Amen.

3 ✧ Scripture Reading

Form A

R. A reading of the Word of God [Exodus 12:21-27].
When the Lord sees the blood on the door, he will
pass over your home.

R. Moses called all the elders of Israel and said to
them, "Go and procure lambs for your families, and
slaughter them as Passover victims. Then take a
bunch of hyssop, and dipping it in the blood that is
in the basin, sprinkle the lintel and the two
doorposts with this blood. But none of you shall go
outdoors until morning. For the Lord will go by,
striking down the Egyptians. Seeing the blood on
the lintel and the two doorposts, the Lord will pass
over that door and not let the destroyer come into
your houses to strike you down.

"You shall observe this as a perpetual ordinance
for yourselves and your descendants. Thus, you
must also observe this rite when you have entered
the land which the Lord will give you as he

promised. When your children ask you, 'What does
this rite of yours mean?' you shall reply, 'This is the
Passover sacrifice of the Lord, who passed over the
houses of the Israelites in Egypt; when he struck
down the Egyptians, he spared our houses.' "

Prayer of Praise (Psalm 40:2, 4ab, 7-8a, 8b-9, 10)

R. Here am I, Lord;
  I come to do your will.

R. I have waited, waited for the Lord,
  and he stooped toward me and heard my cry.
  And he put a new song into my mouth,
  a hymn to our God.

P. **Here am I, Lord;
  I come to do your will.**

R. Sacrifice or oblation you wished not,
  but ears open to obedience you gave me.
  Holocausts or sin-offerings you sought not;
  then said I, "Behold I come."

P. **Here am I, Lord;
  I come to do your will.**

R. In the written scroll it is prescribed for me,
  "To do your will, O my God, is my delight,
  and your law is within my heart!"

P. **Here am I, Lord;
  I come to do your will.**

R. I announced your justice in the vast assembly;
  I did not restrain my lips, as you, O Lord, know.

P. **Here am I, Lord;
  I come to do your will.**

R. A reading from the letter of Paul to the Romans
  [Romans 5:5-11].

Having been justified by his blood, he will be saved from God's anger through him.

R. Hope will not leave us disappointed, because the love of God has been poured out in our hearts through the Holy Spirit who has been given to us. At the appointed time, when we were still powerless, Christ died for us godless men. It is rare that anyone should lay down his life for a just man, though it is barely possible that for a good man someone may have the courage to die. It is precisely in this that God proves his love for us: that while we were still sinners, Christ died for us. Now that we have been justified by his blood, it is all the more certain that we shall be saved by him from God's wrath. For if, when we were God's enemies, we were reconciled to him by the death of his Son, it is all the more certain that we who have been reconciled will be saved by his life. Not only that; we go so far as to make God our boast through our Lord Jesus Christ, through whom we have now received reconciliation.

Alleluia Verse (1 John 4:10)

R. Alleluia, Alleluia, Alleluia.
God first loved us
and sent his Son to take away our sins.

P. **Alleluia, Alleluia, Alleluia.**

Pr. A reading from the holy gospel according to Matthew [Matthew 11:25-30].
I am meek and humble of heart.

Jesus said: "Father, Lord of heaven and earth, to you I offer praise; for what you have hidden from the learned and the clever, you have revealed to the merest children. Father, it is true. You have graciously willed it so. Everything has been given over to me by my Father. No one knows the Son but the Father, and no one knows the Father but the Son — and anyone to whom the Son wishes to reveal him. Come to me all you who are weary and find life burdensome, and I will refresh you. Take my yoke upon your shoulders and learn from me, for I am gentle and humble of heart. Your souls will find rest, for my yoke is easy and my burden light."

Form B

R. A reading from the Book of Exodus [Exodus 24:3-8]. *This is the blood marking the covenant the Lord has made with you.*

R. When Moses came to the people and related all the words and ordinances of the Lord, they all answered with one voice, "We will do everything that the Lord has told us." Moses then wrote down all the words of the Lord and, rising early the next day, he erected at the foot of the mountain an altar and twelve pillars for the twelve tribes of Israel. Then, having sent certain young men of the Israelites to offer holocausts and sacrifice young bulls as peace offerings to the Lord, Moses took half of the blood and put it in large bowls; the other half he splashed on the altar. Taking the book of the covenant, he read it aloud to the people, who answered, "All that the Lord has said, we will heed and do." Then he took the blood and sprinkled it on the people, saying, "This is the blood of the covenant which the Lord has made with you in accordance with all these words of his."

Prayer of Praise (Psalm 23:1-3, 4, 5, 6)

R.   **The Lord is my shepherd;
there is nothing I shall want.**

R.   The Lord is my shepherd; I shall not want.
In verdant pastures he gives me repose;
Beside restful waters he leads me;
he refreshes my soul.

P.   **The Lord is my shepherd;
there is nothing I shall want.**

R.   Only goodness and kindness follow me
all the days of my life;
And I shall dwell in the house of the Lord
for years to come.

P.   **The Lord is my shepherd;
there is nothing I shall want.**

R.   A reading from the Book of Revelation [Revelation
5:6-12].

*You brought us back to God by shedding your blood
for us.*

R.   Between the throne with the four living creatures
and the elders, I, John, saw a Lamb standing, a
Lamb that had been slain. He had seven horns and
seven eyes; these eyes are the seven spirits of God,
sent to all parts of the world. The Lamb came and
received the scroll from the right hand of the One
who sat on the throne. When he had taken the
scroll, the four living creatures and the twenty-four
elders fell down before the Lamb. Along with their
harps, the elders were holding vessels of gold filled
with aromatic spices, which were the prayers of
God's holy people. This is the new hymn they sang:
    "Worthy are you to receive the scroll
    and break open its seals,

for you were slain.
With your blood you purchased for God
men of every race and tongue,
of every people and nation.
You made of them a kingdom,
and priests to serve our God,
and they shall reign on the earth."

As my vision continued, I heard the voices of many
angels who surrounded the throne and the living
creatures and the elders. They were countless in
number, thousands and tens of thousands, and
they all cried out:

"Worthy is the Lamb that was slain
to receive power and riches, wisdom and strength,
honor and glory and praise!"

Alleluia Verse (John 6:51)

R. **Alleluia, Alleluia, Alleluia.**

R. "I am the living bread from heaven, says the Lord; if
anyone eats this bread he will live for ever."

P. **Alleluia, Alleluia, Alleluia.**

Pr. A reading from the holy gospel according to John
[John 19:31-37].

*When they pierced his side with a spear, blood and
water flowed out.*

Since it was the Preparation Day the Jews did not
want to have the bodies left on the cross during the
sabbath, for that sabbath was a solemn feast day.
They asked Pilate that the legs be broken and the
bodies be taken away. Accordingly, the soldiers
came and broke the legs of the men crucified with
Jesus, first of the one, then of the other. When they
came to Jesus and saw that he was already dead,

they did not break his legs. One of the soldiers
thrust a lance into his side, and immediately blood
and water flowed out. (This testimony has been
given by an eyewitness, and his testimony is true.
He tells what he knows is true, so that you may
believe.) These events took place for the fulfillment
of Scripture: "Break none of His bones." There is
still another Scripture passage which says: "They
shall look on Him whom they have pierced."

Form C

R.   A reading from the book of the prophet Hosea
[Hosea 11:lb, 3-4, 8c-9].
My heart is saddened at the thought of parting.

R.   The Lord said:
When Israel was a child I loved him,
out of Egypt I called my son.
Yet it was I who taught Ephraim to walk,
who took them in my arms;
I drew them with human cords,
with bands of love;
I fostered them like one
who raises an infant to his cheeks;
Yet, though I stooped to feed my child,
they did not know that I was their healer.
My heart is overwhelmed,
my pity is stirred.
I will not give vent to my blazing anger,
I will not destroy Ephraim again;
For I am God and not man,
the Holy One present among you;
I will not let the flames consume you.

Prayer of Praise (Psalm 103:1-2, 3-4, 6-7, 8, 10)

P.   **The Lord's kindness is everlasting
to those who fear him.**

R.   Bless the Lord, O my soul;
and all my being, bless his holy name.
Bless the Lord, O my soul,
and forget not all his benefits.

P.   **The Lord's kindness is everlasting
to those who fear him.**

R.   He pardons all your iniquities,
he heals all your ills.
He redeems your life from destruction,
he crowns you with kindness and compassion.

P.   **The Lord's kindness is everlasting
to those who fear him.**

R.   The Lord secures justice
and the right of all the oppressed.
He has made known his ways to Moses,
and his deeds to the children of Israel.

P.   **The Lord's kindness is everlasting
to those who fear him.**

R.   Merciful and gracious is the Lord,
slow to anger and abounding in kindness.
Not according to our sins does he deal with us,
nor does he requite us according to our crimes.

P.   **The Lord's kindness is everlasting
to those who fear him.**

R.   A reading from the first letter of John [1 John 4,
7-16].
We love God because He has loved us first.
Beloved,
let us love one another
because love is of God;

everyone who loves is begotten of God
and has knowledge of God.
The man without love has known nothing of God,
for God is love.
God's love was revealed in our midst in this way:
he sent his only Son to the world
that we might have life through him.
Love, then, consists in this:
not that we have loved God,
but that he has loved us
and has sent his Son as an offering for our sins.
Beloved,
if God has loved us so,
we must have the same love for one another.
No one has ever seen God.
Yet if we love one another
God dwells in us,
and his love is brought to perfection in us.
The way we know we remain in him
and he in us
is that he has given us of his Spirit.
We have seen for ourselves, and can testify,
that the Father has sent the Son as Savior of the world.
When anyone acknowledges that Jesus is the Son of
    God,
God dwells in him
and he in God.
We have come to know and to believe
in the love God has for us.
God is love,
and he who abides in love
abides in God
and God in him.

Alleluia Verse (John 15:9)

P. **Alleluia, Alleluia, Alleluia.**

R. As the Father has loved me, so have I loved you;
remain in my love.

P. **Alleluia, Alleluia, Alleluia.**

Pr. A reading from the holy gospel according to John
[John 15:1-8].

Live in me as I live in you.

Jesus said to his disciples:
"I am the true vine
and my Father is the vinegrower.
He prunes away
every barren branch,
but the fruitful ones
he trims clean
to increase their yield.
You are clean already,
thanks to the word I have spoken to you.
Live on in me, as I do in you.
No more than a branch can bear fruit of itself
apart from the vine,
can you bear fruit
apart from me.
I am the vine, you are the branches.
He who lives in me and I in him,
will produce abundantly,
for apart from me you can do nothing.
A man who does not live in me
is like a withered, rejected branch,
picked up to be thrown in the fire and burnt.
If you live in me,
and my words stay part of you,
you may ask what you will —

43

it will be done for you.
My Father has been glorified
in your bearing much fruit
and becoming my disciples."

4 ✧ Hymn

5 ✧ Homily

6 ✧ Silent Reflection

Note: *The Bible Service ends either with the "Solemn Closing" (below) followed by Benediction, or by Benediction alone (see page 27).*

After Benediction, the Sacrament of Penance can be celebrated so that all parishioners present may have the opportunity to be reconciled with God and His Church.

7 ✧ Litany of the Saints — *sung or recited*

Pr. Lord, have mercy.

P. **Lord, have mercy.**

Pr. Christ, have mercy.

P. **Christ, have mercy.**

Pr. Lord, have mercy.

P. **Lord, have mercy.**

Pr. Holy Mary, Mother of God,

P. **Pray for us.** *(Same response for the following invocations.)*

Pr. St. Michael,
Holy angels of God,
St. John the Baptist,
St. Joseph,
St. Peter and St. Paul,
St. Andrew,
St. John,

St. Mary Magdalene,

St. Stephen,

St. Ignatius,

St. Lawrence,

St. Perpetua and St. Felicity,

St. Agnes,

St. Gregory,

St. Augustine,

St. Athanasius,

St. Basil,

St. Martin,

St. Benedict,

St. Francis and St. Dominic,

St. Francis Xavier,

St. John Vianney,

St. Teresa of Ávila,

St. Catherine of Siena,

All holy men and women,

Lord, be merciful.

P.   **Lord, save your people.** *(Same response for the following invocations.)*

Pr.   From all evil,

From every sin,

From everlasting death,

By your coming as man,

By your death and rising to new life,

By your gift of the Holy Spirit,

Be merciful to us sinners.

P.   **Lord, hear our prayer.** *(Same response for the following invocations.)*

Guide and protect your holy Church,

Keep our pope and all the clergy in faithful service to your Church,

Bring all peoples together in trust and peace,

Strengthen us in your service.

Pr. Christ, hear us.

P. **Christ, hear us.**

Pr. Lord Jesus, hear our prayer.

P. **Lord Jesus, hear our prayer.**

Pr. Let us pray.

From you, Lord, comes holiness in our desires, right thinking in our plans, and justice in our actions. Grant your children that peace which the world cannot give; then our hearts will be devoted to your laws, we shall be delivered from the terrors of war, and under your protection we shall be able to live in tranquility. Amen.

Alternative prayer:

Lord Jesus Christ, we worship you living among us in the sacrament of your body and blood. May we offer to our Father in heaven a solemn pledge of undivided love. May we offer to our brothers and sisters a life poured out in loving service of that kingdom where you live with the Father and the Holy Spirit, one God, for ever and ever.

8 ✧ Procession

9 ✧ Hymn
Sing, My Tongue, the Savior's Glory

1. Sing, my tongue, the Savior's glory,
   Of His flesh the mystery sing;
   Of the blood all price exceeding,
   Shed by our immortal King,
   Destined for the world's redemption,
   From a noble womb to spring.

2. Of a pure and spotless Virgin
   Born for us on earth below,

He, as Man, with man conversing,
Stayed, the seeds of truth to sow;
Then He closed in solemn order
Wondrously His life of woe.

3. On the night of that last supper
Seated with His chosen band,
He, the Paschal Victim, eating,
First fulfills the Law's command;
Then as food to His apostles
Gives Himself with His own hand.

4. Word made Flesh, the bread of nature
By His word to flesh He turns:
Wine into His Blood He changes,
What though sense no change discerns!
Only be the heart in earnest,
Faith her lesson quickly learns.

5. Down in adoration falling,
Lo! the Sacred Host we hail;
Lo! o'er ancient forms departing,
Newer rites of grace prevail;
Faith for all defects supplying
Where the feeble senses fail.

6. To the everlasting Father,
And the Son who reigns on high,
With the Spirit blest proceeding
Forth from each eternally,
Be salvation, honor, blessing,
Might and endless majesty.

Benediction follows (see page 27).

HYMNS

1 ❦ Father, We Thank Thee

From the Didache, c. 110; Louis Bourgeois, 1543 (tr. F. Bland Tucker)

1. Father, we thank Thee who hast planted
   Thy Holy Name within our hearts.
   Knowledge and faith and life immortal
   Jesus, thy Son, to us imparts.
   Thou, Lord, didst make all for thy pleasure,
   Didst give man food for all his days.
   Giving in Christ the Bread eternal;
   Thine is the power, be thine the praise.

2. Watch o'er Thy Church, O Lord, in mercy,
   Save it from evil, guard it still;
   Perfect it in Thy love, unite it,
   Cleansed and conformed unto Thy will.
   As grain, once scattered on the hillsides,
   Was in this broken bread made one,
   So from all lands Thy Church be gathered
   Into Thy kingdom by Thy Son.

(Used by permission of the Church Pension Fund.)

2 ❦ Holy God, We Praise Thy Name

Ignaz Franz, c. 1774 (tr. C. Walworth, 1820-1900, alt.)

1. Holy God, we praise thy Name;
   Lord of all, we bow before thee;
   All on earth thy rule acclaim,
   All in heav'n above adore thee;
   //Infinite, thy vast domain,
   Everlasting is thy reign.//

2. Hark! the loud celestial hymn
   Angel choirs above are raising;
   Cherubim and Seraphim
   In unceasing chorus praising;
   //Fill the heav'ns with sweet accord,
   Holy, holy, holy Lord!//

3 ❦ O! What Could My Jesus Do More

1. O! what could my Jesus do more,
   Or what greater blessings impart,
   O silence my soul and adore,
   And press Him still nearer Thy heart.
2. 'Tis here from my labor I'll rest,
   Since He makes my poor heart His abode.
   To Him all my cares I'll address,
   And speak to the heart of my God.
3. In life and in death Thou art mine.
   My Savior, I'm sealed with Thy blood
   Till eternity on me doth shine,
   I'll live on the flesh of my God.
4. In Jesus triumphant I'll live,
   In Jesus triumphant I'll die.
   The terrors of death calmly brave,
   On His bosom breathe out my last sigh.

4 ❦ Soul of My Savior

1. Soul of my Savior, sanctify my breast,
   Body of Christ, be Thou my saving Guest;
   Blood of my Savior, bathe me in Thy tide,
   Wash me, ye waters, gushing from His Side.
2. Strength and protection, may Thy Passion be,
   O Blessed Jesus, hear and answer me;
   Deep in Thy Wounds, Lord, hide and shelter me;
   So shall I never, never part from Thee.
3. Guard and defend me from the foe malign
   In death's dread moments make me only Thine.
   Call me, and bid me come to Thee that day
   Where I may praise Thee with Thy Saints for aye.

5 ❦ O God of Loveliness

1. O God of loveliness,
   O Lord of Heaven above,
   How worthy to possess

49

My heart's devoted love!
So sweet Thy Countenance,
So gracious to behold,
That one, and only glance
To me were bliss untold.

2. Thou art blest Three in One,
Yet undivided still;
Thou art that One alone
Whose love my heart can fill,
The heavens and earth below,
Were fashioned by Thy Word;
How admirable art Thou,
My ever dearest Lord.

3. O loveliness supreme,
And beauty infinite,
O ever flowing stream,
And ocean of delight;
O life by which I live,
My truest life above,
To You alone I give
My undivided love.

6 ✢ Lord, Who at Your First Eucharist Did Pray

W. H. Turton; W. H. Monk

1. Lord, who at Your first Eucharist did pray
That all Your Church might be forever one,
Grant us at every Eucharist to say
With longing heart and soul, "Your will be done."
O may we all one bread, one body be,
Through this blest Sacrament of Unity.

2. For all Thy Church, O Lord, we intercede;
Make Thou our sad divisions soon to cease;
Draw us the nearer each to each, we plead,
By drawing all to Thee, O Prince of Peace:
Thus may we all . . .

3. So, Lord, at length when sacraments shall cease,
   May we be one with all Thy Church above,
   One with Thy saints in one unbroken peace,
   One with Thy saints in one unbounded love:
   More blessed still, in peace and love to be
   One with the Trinity in Unity.

7 ℣ O Esca Viatorum*

1. O esca viatorum,
   O Panis Angelorum,
   O Manna Coelitum:
   Esurientes Ciba
   Dulcedine non priva
   Corda quaerentium,
   Corda quaerentium.
2. O lympha, fons amoris
   Qui puro Salvatoris
   E corde Profluis;
   Te sitientes pota
   His, una sufficis,
   His, una sufficis.

*O Food That Weary Pilgrims Love

1. O Food that weary pilgrims love,
   O Bread of Angel hosts above,
   O Manna of the Saints:
   The hungry soul would feed on Thee,
   Ne'er may the heart unsolaced be
   Which for Thy sweetness faints.
2. O fount of love, O cleansing tide,
   Which from the Savior's pierced side,
   And Sacred Heart does flow;
   Be ours to drink from Thy pure rill,
   Which only can our spirits fill,
   And all we need bestow.

8 ❦ Jesus, My Lord, My God

1. Jesus, my Lord, my God, my All,
   How can I love Thee as I ought?
   And how revere this wondrous gift,
   So far surpassing hope and thought.
   Chorus:
   Sweet Sacrament! we Thee adore,
   //O make us love Thee more and more.//
2. Had I but Mary's sinless Heart,
   To love Thee with, my dearest King,
   O with what bursts of fervent praise,
   Thy goodness Jesus, would I sing.
   Repeat chorus

9 ❦ To Jesus' Heart All Burning

1. To Jesus' Heart all burning
   With fervent love for man,
   My heart with fondest yearning
   Shall raise the joyful strain.
2. While ages course along,
   Blest be with loudest song
   The Sacred Heart of Jesus
   By ev'ry heart and tongue.
3. O Heart for me on fire,
   With love no man can speak.
   My yet untold desire,
   God gives me for Thy sake.

10 ❦ Salve Regina*

Salve Regina, Mater misericordiae,
Vita, dulcedo, et spes nostra, salve.
Ad te clamamus, exsules, filii Evae
Ad te suspiramus, gementes et flentes
In hac lacrimarum valle.
Eia ergo, Advocata nostra,
Illos tuos misericordes oculos

Ad nos converte.
Et Iesum, benedictum fructum ventris tui
Nobis post hoc exsilium ostende.
O clemens, O pia, O dulcis Virgo Maria.

*Hail, Holy Queen

Hail, Holy Queen, Mother of Mercy, hail,
Our life, our sweetness, and our hope!
To you do we cry, poor banished children of Eve.
To you do we send up our sighs, mourning
And weeping in this vale of tears.
Turn then, most gracious Advocate,
Your eyes of mercy toward us;
And after this our exile,
Show us the Blessed Fruit of your womb, Jesus.
O clement, O loving, O sweet Virgin Mary!

11 ❦ Come, Holy Ghost

Rabanus Maurus, 776-856(?) (tr. Edward Caswall, 1849 alt.)

1. Come Holy Ghost, Creator blest,
   And in our hearts take up thy rest;
   Come with thy grace and heav'nly aid
   //To fill the hearts which Thou hast made.//

2. O Comfort blest, to thee we cry,
   Thou heav'nly Gift of God most High;
   Thou Font of life, and Fire of love,
   //And sweet Anointing from above.//

3. Praise be to Thee, Father and Son,
   And Holy Spirit, Three in One:
   And may the Son on us bestow
   //The gifts that from the Spirit flow.//

12 ❦ I Love Thee, O Mary

1. I love thee, O Mary!
   Thy name I revere,
   Sweet Virgin of virgins,

Our Lady most dear!
My heart with devotion
Turns ever to thee;
For thou art my beacon
On life's stormy sea!

2. I love thee, O Mary!
Thy praise I proclaim;
In joy and in sorrow,
I call on thy name.
To thee, O sweet Mother,
For refuge I fly,
When dangers surround me
And tempests are nigh.

13 ❦ See Us, Lord, About Your Altar

J. Greally, S.J., alt.

1. See us, Lord, about your altar,
Though so many, we are one;
Many souls by love united
In the heart of Christ, your Son.

2. Hear our prayers, O loving Father,
Hear in them your Son, Our Lord;
Hear Him speak our love and worship
As we sing with one accord.

3. Once were seen the blood and water;
Now is seen but bread and wine;
Once in human form He suffered,
Now His form is but a sign.

Eucharistic Exposition and Benediction with Evening Prayer

A. Introduction

As the minister and acolytes come to the altar, an appropriate evening prayer-hymn is sung (such as "Sing, My Tongue, the Savior's Glory," page 46).

The sacrament is brought to the altar and placed in the monstrance upon the table of the altar.

The minister then incenses the sacrament.

B. Adoration

1. Psalmody

After a brief period of silent adoration, all are seated while the following psalm antiphons are said.

Ant. 1 The Lord is compassionate; he gives food to those who fear him as a remembrance of his great deeds.

Psalm 111
I will thank the Lord with all my heart
in the meeting of the just and their assembly.
Great are the works of the Lord;
to be pondered by all who love them.
Majestic and glorious his work,
his justice stands firm for ever.
He makes us remember his wonders.
The Lord is compassion and love.
He gives food to those who fear him;
keeps his covenant ever in mind.
He has shown his might to his people
by giving them the lands of the nations.
His works are justice and truth:
his precepts are all of them sure,

standing firm for ever and ever:
they are made in uprightness and truth.
He has sent deliverance to his people
and established his covenant for ever.
Holy his name, to be feared.
To fear the Lord is the first stage of wisdom;
all who do so prove themselves wise.
His praise shall last for ever!

Psalm-prayer:
Merciful and gentle Lord, you are the crowning glory of
all the saints. Give us, your children, the gift of
obedience which is the beginning of wisdom, so that we
may do what you command and be filled with your
mercy.

Ant. 2 The Lord brings peace to his Church, and fills
us with the finest wheat.

Psalm 147:12-20
O praise the Lord, Jerusalem!
Zion, praise your God!
He has strengthened the bars of your gates,
he has blessed the children within you.
He established peace on your borders,
he feeds you with finest wheat.
He sends out his word to the earth
and swiftly runs his command.
He showers down snow white as wool,
he scatters hoar-frost like ashes.
He hurls down hailstones like crumbs.
The waters are frozen at his touch;
he sends forth his word and it melts them:
at the breath of his mouth the waters flow.
He makes his word known to Jacob,

to Israel his laws and decrees.
He has not dealt thus with other nations;
he has not taught them his decrees.

Psalm-prayer:
Lord, you established peace within the borders of
Jerusalem. Give the fullness of peace now to your
faithful people. May peace rule us in this life and
possess us in eternal life. You are about to fill us with
the best of wheat; grant that what we see dimly now as
in a mirror, we may come to perceive clearly in the
brightness of your truth.

Ant. 3 Truly I say to you: Moses did not give you the
bread from heaven; my Father gives you the true bread
from heaven, alleluia.

Canticle — Revelation 11:17-18, 12:10-12
We praise you, the Lord God Almighty,
who is and who was.
You have assumed your great power,
you have begun your reign.
The nations have raged in anger,
but then came your day of wrath
and the moment to judge the dead:
The time to reward your servants the prophets
and the holy ones who revere you,
the great and the small alike.
Now have salvation and power come,
the reign of our God and the authority
of his Anointed One.
For the accuser of our brothers is cast out,
who night and day accused them before God.
They defeated him by the blood of the Lamb
and by the word of their testimony;

love for life did not deter them from death.
So rejoice, you heavens,
and you that dwell therein!

2. Reading
*A selection may be made from the Lectionary for Mass,
or the following reading (1 Corinthians 10:16-17) may be
used:*

Is not the cup of blessing we bless a sharing in the
blood of Christ? And is not the bread we break a sharing
in the body of Christ? Because the loaf of bread is one,
we, many though we are, are one body, for we all partake
of the one loaf.

3. Homily
*The celebrant draws his homily from the Scripture
passage just proclaimed.*

4. Period of Silent Reflection

5. Canticle of Mary

6. Intercessions
Pr. Christ invites all to the supper in which he gives
his body and blood for the life of the world. Let us
ask him:

**P. Christ, the bread of heaven, grant us
everlasting life.**

Pr. Christ, Son of the living God, you commanded that
this thanksgiving meal be done in memory of you,
~ enrich your Church through the faithful
celebration of these mysteries.

**P. Christ, the bread of heaven, grant us
everlasting life.**

Pr. Christ, eternal priest of the Most High, you have

commanded your priests to offer your sacraments, ~ may they help them to exemplify in their lives the meaning of the sacred mysteries which they celebrate.

P. Christ, the bread of heaven, grant us everlasting life.

Pr. Christ, bread from heaven, you form one body out of all who partake of the one bread, ~ refresh all who believe in you with harmony and peace.

P. Christ, the bread of heaven, grant us everlasting life.

Pr. Christ, through your bread you offer the promise of immortality and the pledge of future resurrection, ~ restore health to the sick and living hope to sinners.

P. Christ, the bread of heaven, grant us everlasting life.

Pr. Christ, our king who is to come, you commanded that the mysteries which proclaim your death be celebrated until you return, ~ grant that all who die in you may share in your resurrection.

P. Christ, the bread of heaven, grant us everlasting life.

C. Benediction

Toward the end of the exposition, the priest or deacon goes to the altar, genuflects, and kneels. A hymn or eucharistic song is sung while the minister incenses the sacrament.

1. Song
An appropriate hymn, such as "Down in Adoration Falling," page 27, is sung.

2. Prayer

After the song, the minister stands and sings (or says) the concluding prayer. All respond: "Amen."

3. Blessing

The priest, or in the absence of a priest, the deacon, then blesses the people with the sacrament.

D. Reposition

After the blessing the priest or deacon who gave the blessing (or another priest or deacon) replaces the blessed sacrament in the tabernacle and genuflects. Meanwhile the people may sing or say an acclamation; and the minister then leaves.

Eucharistic Exposition and Benediction (Model Service)

A. Introduction

As the minister and acolytes come to the altar, a eucharistic hymn (such as "O Saving Victim," page 10) may be sung. The sacrament is brought to the altar and placed in the monstrance upon the table of the altar. The minister then incenses the sacrament.

B. Adoration

After a period of silent adoration, all are seated as the reader goes to the lectern for the first reading.

1. First Reading: Exodus 16:2-4, 12-15 (Lect. no. 904.2), "The Lord will rain bread on us from heaven."

2. Responsorial Psalm: Psalm 34:2-3, 4-5, 6-7, 8-9, 17-18, 19, and 23 (Lect. no. 912.5).

P. **Taste and see the goodness of the Lord.**

Pr. I will bless the Lord at all times;
his praise shall be ever in my mouth.
Let my soul glory in the Lord;
the lowly will hear me and be glad.

P. **Taste and see the goodness of the Lord.**

Pr. Glorify the Lord with me,
let us together extol his name.
I sought the Lord, and he answered me
and delivered me from all my fears.

P. **Taste and see the goodness of the Lord.**

Pr. Look to him that you may be radiant with joy,
and your faces may not blush with shame.

When the afflicted man called out, the Lord heard,
and from all his distress he saved him.

P. Taste and see the goodness of the Lord.

Pr. The angel of the Lord encamps
around those who fear him, and delivers them.
Taste and see how good the Lord is;
happy the man who takes refuge in him.

P. Taste and see the goodness of the Lord.

Pr. The Lord confronts the evildoers,
to destroy remembrance of them from the earth.
When the just cry out, the Lord hears them,
and from all their distress he rescues them.

P. Taste and see the goodness of the Lord.

Pr. The Lord is close to the brokenhearted;
and those who are crushed in spirit he saves.
The Lord redeems the lives of his servants;
no one incurs guilt who takes refuge in him.

P. Taste and see the goodness of the Lord.

3. Gospel: John 6:24-35 (Lect. no. 909.5).
"If you come to me, you will never be hungry. He who
believes in me will never know thirst."

4. Homily: The priest or deacon draws his homily
from the contents of the scripture passages proclaimed.

(In place of the homily, a reading from one of the
Church fathers may be selected. See the non-scriptural
reading presented in the *Liturgy of the Hours* for the
solemnity of Corpus Christi [Volume III, page 610].)

5. Period of Silent Reflection

6. Intercessions

The minister leads the community in a series of